HILLARY SAYS!

An Off-Color Hillary Clinton Coloring Book

Tom F. O'Leary

D1529606

gumdrop*press*

Silver Spring, Maryland

Visit us at gumdroppress.com!

ISBN-13: 978-0692548431 (Gumdrop Press)

ISBN-10: 0692548432

"Oftentimes when you face such an overwhelming challenge as global climate change, it can be somewhat daunting - it's kind of like trying to lose weight, which I know something about."

"We're going to take things away from you on behalf of the common good."

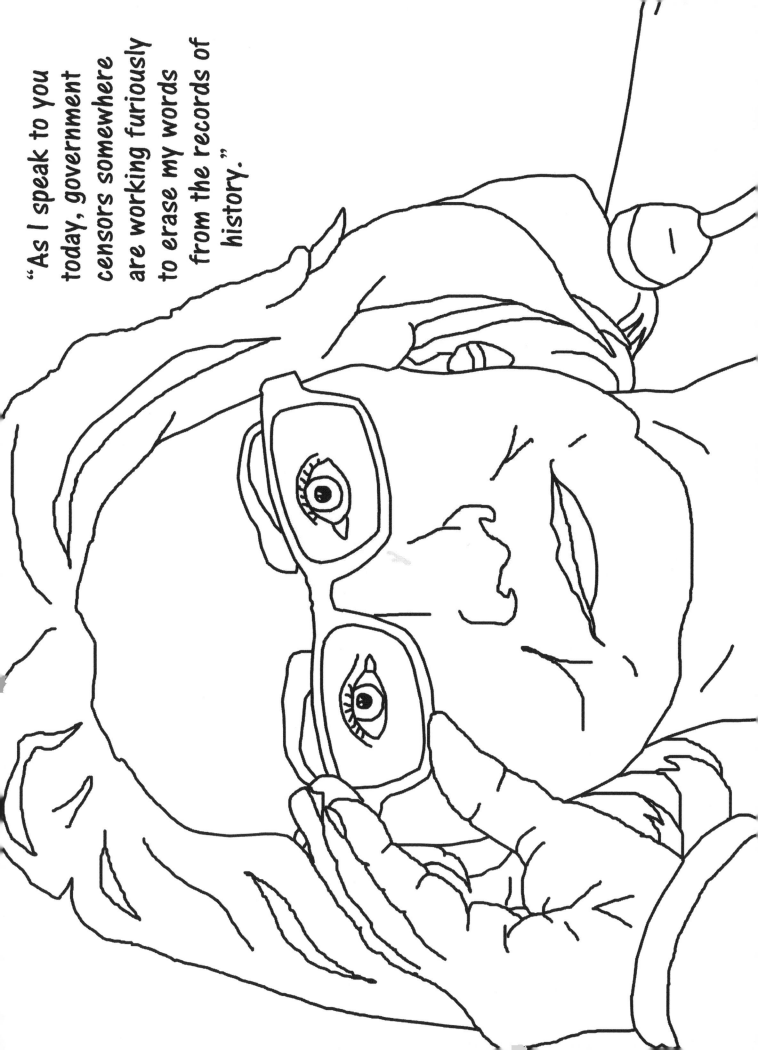

"As I speak to you today, government censors somewhere are working furiously to erase my words from the records of history."

"I'm not going to have some reporters pawing through our papers. We are the president."

"I have known several presidents quite well, including my husband."

"God bless the America we are trying to create."

"If you have guns in your home, tell your parents to keep them away from you and your friends and your little brothers and sisters."

"I suppose I could have stayed home and baked cookies and had teas."

"If I want to knock a story off the front page, I just change my hairstyle."

"I have absolutely no interest in running for president again. None. None."

"In my White House, we will know who wears the pantsuits."

"I remember landing under sniper fire."

"The truth is that sometimes it is hard even for me to recognize the Hillary Clinton that other people see."

.

"I am not going to comment on what I did or did not say back in the late '90s."

"I think I'm very hardheaded."

"The American people are tired of liars and people who pretend to be something they're not."

"Don't let anybody tell you it's corporations and businesses create jobs."

"I believe in transparency."

"I wish I had some stock in a scrunchie company."

52298107R00025

Made in the USA
Lexington, KY
23 May 2016